# Prehistoric Animals

RUPERT OLIVER

Illustrated by

BERNARD LONG

GALLERY BOOKS
An Imprint of W. H. Smith Publishers Inc.
112 Madison Avenue
New York City 10016

As can be seen by the two examples on these pages, not all members of the elephant family were the same size. This is the Imperial mammoth which was much larger than the *Palaeoloxodon falconeri* opposite.

First published in Great Britain in 1982 by
Hodder and Stoughton Children's Books

This edition published in 1990 by Gallery Books
An imprint of W.H. Smith Publishers Inc.
112 Madison Avenue
New York 10016

By arrangement with Octopus Books Limited

Copyright © 1982 Martspress Ltd.

All rights reserved

ISBN 0-8317-7137-2

Printed in Portugal

# Contents

| | |
|---|---|
| The Early Species | 8 |
| In the Sea and in the Air | 12 |
| Some Early Giants | 12 |
| On the Plains | 20 |
| Ancient Relatives of today's Mammals | 27 |
| The Sabre-toothed Tiger | 35 |
| In the Southern Hemisphere | 39 |
| Prehistoric Animals of Australia | 42 |
| The Mighty Mastodon | 44 |
| The Ice Ages | 48 |
| The Woolly Mammals | 54 |
| Pronunciations | 60 |

# Prehistoric Animals

## The Early Species

The world we live in today is a world of mammals. A mammal is a warm-blooded animal which during its early life feeds on its mother's milk.

Mankind itself is a species of mammal and most of the animals alive today are mammals, from the largest elephant to the tiniest mouse. Though there are also birds and reptiles, there can be no doubt that mammals dominate the earth.

The world one hundred and fifty million years ago was very different. Then the ground shook to the thudding footsteps of the mighty dinosaurs.

How this strange world, dominated by dinosaurs, became our world, dominated by mammals, is the story of this book.

While the dinosaurs roamed the world, there scurried along small insignificant looking creatures which, unlike the dinosaurs, were covered in hair. They were mammals.

We know this, not because man was there to see it (he was not to appear for a very long time), but because scientists have found the bones of these creatures hidden in rocks that were formed all

those years ago. Bones preserved in this way are known as fossils.

When the fossil of one of these early primitive mammals was discovered, scientists gave to it the name of *Deltatheridium*. It was not the earliest mammal, for mammals had already been around for several million years.

The *Deltatheridium* lived by eating insects and small animals. Only ten centimetres long, it was a member of the group that evolved into all later mammals and for this reason it is important.

When we say that an animal has evolved, we mean that over the centuries a certain type of animal has changed in appearance until at last it looks little or nothing like the creature from which it is descended. This process has gone on all through the history of life

The *Deltatheridium* was one of the early mammals which lived millions of years ago in the time of the dinosaurs.

and still continues today. You will not see a species change, however, for it is a very slow process.

The idea of evolution was first realised by the great scientist Charles Darwin.

The mammals may have stayed for ever in the shadows of the dinosaurs had not something mysterious happened. It is a mystery that even today scientists are at a loss to explain – the dinosaurs vanished. In rocks less than sixty-five million years old there are no dinosaur fossils. Many theories have been put forward to explain this strange disappearance. Some people think that perhaps there was a sudden and drastic change in climate that killed the dinosaurs, some that there was possibly a mighty disaster, such as a comet crashing to earth, but no-one as yet knows.

It took a long time for the mammals to take advantage of the death of the dinosaurs but within ten million years of that startling event (that is fifty-six million years ago) there were such creatures as those depicted here.

Already there were different mammal families, just as today there are the horse and dog families.

The *Oxyaena lupina*, for example, belonged to a family called by today's scientists Creodonta while the *Phenacodus primaevus* belonged to the family known as Condylarthra.

These two animals lived in North America. Both were still primitive compared with today's mammals but they lived very different lives.

The *Oxyaena*, like all Creodonts, was a meat eater. Its fossil teeth were sharp and ideal for slicing up lumps of flesh. Its strong front legs suggest that when hunting for food it pounced on its prey.

The *Phenacodus*, on the other hand, was no meat eater. This herbivore (which means plant eater) was fifty-five centimetres tall and it is interesting to note that it shows characteristics of both its ancestors and its descendants.

From its fossils it is obvious that it had the same ancestor as the Creodonts for its skull was small and long while its legs were short and sturdy.

There is no doubt though that the *Phenacodus* lived on plants, for the teeth of this early mammal were beginning to lose the sharpness of the teeth of a

The *Phenacodus*, a gentle plant eater, would have been an easy prey for the wily hunter, the *Oxyaena*.

carnivore (which means flesh eater) and becoming the large sturdy grinders needed to deal with plants.

Unlike the *Oxyaena*, the *Phenacodus* did not become extinct without leaving any descendants for it is generally believed that the *Phenacodus*, or some similar animal, was the ancestor of all the ungulates, that is animals with hooves, such as horses and cows. But that lay a long way ahead, for it walked on the soles of its feet and not on its toes.

### In the Sea and in the Air

After the dinosaurs disappeared, the mammals – as for example the *Phenacodus* and the *Oxyaena* – were not only free to start taking over the roles of large herbivores and carnivores from the dinosaurs but the chance to adapt to the seas was also afforded them.

It is surprising that perhaps the earliest mammal to take to the water was not an ancestor of the common present-day water-living mammals, such as the whales or seals, but of the manatee, a sluggish and very primitive present-day mammal that has changed very little since it first took to the waters many millions of years ago.

The *Protosiren*, pictured opposite, was one of these prehistoric creatures.

This group of animals has always been satisfied to spend a quiet life feeding on soft plants that it finds in the quiet coves and estuaries where it passes its life.

The *Protosiren* must have lived a very similar life to the present-day manatee, congregating in small groups to feed.

Examining the fossils of these early creatures, it is possible to discern some strong similarities to the fossils of early elephants.

It seems therefore that these two quite different groups of present-day mam-

This peculiar looking animal is the sluggish *Protosiren*, an extinct relative of the modern Manatee.

mals, the elephants and the manatees, have evolved from the same primitive group.

The dinosaurs were not the only animals to suffer extinction at that far-distant time, for great numbers of species of shellfish also vanished and the species of microscopic creatures were greatly reduced.

More important, though, to the story of the mammals is the fact that the types of plants in the world were changing. For millions of years the only plants growing were ferns and conifers. But towards the end of the dinosaur age they diminished, which left the way open for the flowering plants.

The new plants were very varied and successful and soon the flowering species dominated the world's flora.

The rise of the mammals took place in a world in which plants were much tougher than before, and this meant that those mammals which chose to eat plants needed very strong teeth capable of grinding the plants.

During the Eocene Era, that is about fifty million years ago, the first mammals were taking to the air in the form of bats. The earliest bat of which we know has been named *Icaronycteris* and some of these can be seen on page 14.

Fossils of the *Icaronycteris* have been discovered in rocks, perfectly preserved.

### Some Early Giants

During the Eocene period there lived an important group of mammals, today known as the Uintatheres.

This group had evolved into large herbivores but they were still not as

advanced as today's more familiar animals that have evolved to fill the same "niche" in life, by eating the same food and living in the same way.

The largest of this group was the *Uintatherium mirabile* which, at about three metres long, was just the same size as a present-day African rhinoceros.

It did not, however, live in exactly the same way as the African rhinoceros for its teeth show us that it ate soft plants it found near water in damp forests, whereas the African rhinoceros of today lives in open grasslands.

The most striking features of the *Uintatherium* must surely have been the knobs on its head. It is not really known for what purpose the *Uintatherium* would have used them but we can make a good guess at the use it made of the curved tusks that grew from its upper jaw.

To begin with, they probably evolved to help the huge beast get a firm grip on the plants it ate as it pulled them up out of the ground. However, as the tusks were larger in males than in females, it is reasonable to assume that they were used in fights between rival males, perhaps over territory.

The *Uintatherium* had large spreading feet that helped it to walk on the mud it had to cross to reach its food of soft aquatic plants, as we call plants that grow in water.

Although with its wide feet and strong tusk-like canines, the *Uintatherium* was well suited to its life as a sluggish browser in swamps or along rivers, it was the last, as well as the largest, of the Uintatheres.

These creatures had evolved by growing larger, but at the cost of being left out of the mainstream of evolution. This was eventually to lead to their disappearance about forty million years ago when more advanced mammals were coming along to take their place.

Indeed at the same time that the doomed Uintatheres were in their heyday in North America, there was a much smaller animal living in the swamps of North Africa.

This creature was the ancestor of one of the most successful groups of animals that our world has seen. Known today as the *Moeritherium lyonsi*, it was the forerunner of the elephants.

It is perhaps difficult to imagine anything less like today's mighty elephant than this creature.

Apart from its size, (it was only seventy centimetres tall), it did not have a trunk nor the large tusks so characteristic of the modern elephant. But today's scientists believe that the *Moeritherium*, or at least something very much like it, was in time to evolve into the large range of elephants that were later to inhabit most parts of the globe.

The *Moeritherium* is thought to have lived much as the hippopotamus does today.

By spending long periods of the day in the cool waters of lakes and rivers, the *Moeritherium* would have been comparatively safe from the prowling carnivores of the time, hungry flesh eaters that would no doubt have made a tasty meal of the bulky animal.

While spending most of its time in the water, the *Moeritherium* did not find its food there. It sought its diet on the river banks and nearby meadows.

Like today's hippopotamus it may have preferred to stay in the cool water during the day, only venturing to leave the cool depths in the darkness of night.

Although the *Moeritherium* did not have a trunk, it did have a muscular lip which later evolved into the trunk so that the beast was able to reach higher tree-branches for food.

The teeth of this animal show the link with later elephants for, although it lacked the typical tusks, the incisors of both the upper and lower jaws were much enlarged into strong peg teeth.

It should not be thought that the modern African and Indian elephants are the high point of the elephants' evolution just because we see them today.

Fifty million years ago the *Uintatherium*, a large ugly swamp dweller, had evolved as had the early bat, the *Icaronycteris*.

Present-day elephants are just the remnants of a mighty family that was in its full glory some millions of years ago.

Then there were not just the true elephants, but mastodons and mammoths as well, with many species of each roaming over India and most of Asia as well as America, Africa and Europe.

We must now move to Asia where at about the same time as, or a little later than, the *Moeritherium*, there lived a most formidable creature.

This newcomer to our story was the animal that modern scientists have named the *Andrewsarchus mongoliensis*. Its fossils were first found in Mongolia.

The *Andrewsarchus* was a carnivore, all of four metres long. It is famous today mainly for having possessed the largest skull of any known mammal carnivore, measuring eighty centimetres.

Like the *Oxyaena* (that lived earlier in North America) the *Andrewsarchus* was a member of the Creodont family, the first group to take to eating the flesh of other animals with any success.

Apart from its big frame, the *Andrewsarchus* was a very typical Creodont. The Creodonts were meat eaters, but they were not as specialised as today's carnivores.

The *Andrewsarchus* probably ate anything edible that came its way. Its sheer size would have enabled it to overcome large prey, using its massive incisors, but its teeth indicate that it had probably not lost its taste for smaller animals.

Perhaps surprising is that the *Andrewsarchus* is believed to have feasted on

The *Moeritherium* lived over forty million years ago. Though it may be the ancestor of the elephant it was only seventy centimetres tall.

berries and other types of vegetation.

But as other animals developed and specialised, they slowly overtook the Creodonts in every area of feeding.

More cunning carnivores appeared while the hoofed animals were far better at browsing on the bushes for food.

So it was that the whole group of Creodonts found that their niche in the food chain had been taken over by various other animals.

Since they could not adapt to find a new way of life the entire group, including the formidable *Andrewsarchus*, became extinct.

Not all the early flesh eaters died out. One group, that modern scientists have called the Miacids, survived. From them are descended the cats and dogs of later times, including the savage lions and wolves we know today.

The *Andrewsarchus* had the largest skull of any meat-eating mammal, the skull measuring eighty-four centimetres.

In the days when the proud Pharaohs ruled Ancient Egypt there lived a Queen by the name of Arsinoe. A great religious centre was built for her near the present-day desert basin called Fayum. What, you may ask, has this to do with prehistoric animals? Well, a group of scientific seekers of fossils found some mysterious bones near the same Egyptian depression of Fayum, and one of them decided to name this hitherto unknown animal after the Queen.

*Arsinotherium zitteli* was the name given to the beast.

It stood nearly two metres tall and was about three metres long when it was alive thirty-five million years ago. The most striking and dramatic feature of

The *Arsinotherium*, which is named after a Queen of Ancient Egypt, may look like a rhinoceros but it was not related.

this creature was surely its huge horns.

Although in appearance it may well have looked like a modern rhinoceros, it was in no way related to it. Indeed those big horns, so much like those of a rhinoceros, were quite different. The horns of today's rhinoceros are in fact matted hair but the wicked-looking horns on this long extinct creature were bone.

While on the one hand we know that this large beast was not related to the rhinoceros, on the other we are not very sure to what it *was* actually related.

It just seems to have appeared and disappeared in the forests of North Africa all those millions of years ago. Although the Fayum Depression is today desertland, in prehistoric days great forests covered the area.

Although we may not know about the ancestors of the *Arsinotherium*, its fossil remains tell us quite a lot.

For instance, despite the fierce appearance of its horns, it was more than likely a gentle vegetarian that lived on the plants it found in the damp forests where it seems to have spent its life. We can tell this from its teeth.

Then, too, from a study of its leg bones we learn that it was more than likely a slow-moving animal which probably had little need to run fast to escape other beasts, hungry for its flesh. Those two great horns would have helped it to protect itself.

About thirty-two million years ago, the *Arsinotherium*, which, so far as we have been able to discover, was the largest creature in Africa at the time, became extinct.

No remains of descendants have ever been found by scientists. It would seem that it simply vanished from the Earth.

Perhaps some day discoveries may be made that afford an answer to the riddle for, from time to time, new finds are made in the field of palaeontology, that is, the study of extinct forms of life.

We must now move hundreds of miles from the haunts of the *Arsinotherium* to the old hunting grounds of the *Andrewsarchus* (see page 17). But that animal had been dead and gone for some millions of years by the time the next subjects in our book walked the wild plains of present-day Mongolia.

Whereas the *Arsinotherium* looked like a rhinoceros but was not, the mighty *Indricotherium parvum* was a rhinoceros.

Strangely, though, as you can see from the illustration on the next two pages, this long-necked giant did not look anything like the modern rhinoceros.

To start with, it was enormous. It stood a full five and a half metres tall at the shoulder and a good deal taller than that when it raised its head.

This great height, together with its length of eight metres, made it the largest land mammal of its day. More than that, it is still the largest land mammal of which science is aware, far larger than the largest elephants of today.

It is a good example of how one group of animals may diversify to fill many niches in life. Whilst other members of the rhinoceros family remained small, one branch grew larger and larger and ended in this huge creature of the plains.

There is no doubt that the size and long neck of this strange beast evolved as a direct result of its search for food.

Its teeth indicate that it ate the leaves and twigs of trees that were scattered about on the plains where it lived.

Not only were its teeth designed for this type of food but its very mobile upper lip was no doubt of great use in the delicate task of plucking leaves from the trees.

In the constant search for more and more food, the ancestors of the *Indricotherium* grew taller and so the animal was able to take advantage of the leaves growing on the tops of trees, leaves that other creatures could not reach.

It is believed that these animals wandered the plains in small herds, moving from one clump of trees to another.

Like other prehistoric animals, the *Indricotherium* and its relatives became extinct because they could not evolve and adapt themselves to a new way of life. They were just too specialised to a life of tree-browsing.

## On the Plains

While Asia was witnessing the end of one evolutionary line, yet another was coming to an end in North America.

This was the line of the family known as Titanotheridae.

In the early days of fossil collecting, large expeditions were mounted in the Western States of America to discover and bring back fossils and it was at this time that the fossils of the Titanotheridae were first discovered by scientists.

But the fossils had been known to the local Indians for some time, though they had no idea what they really were.

That warlike tribe, the Sioux, therefore explained these strange bones as belonging to the great Thunder Horse that leaped from the skies during heavy storms and whose hooves made the rolling sound of thunder.

But they bore no resemblance to, and were certainly not, horses, as you can

The *Indricotherium* was larger than any other land mammal before or since. It was about five and a half metres tall at the shoulder.

The huge, lumbering *Brontotherium* lived in North America along with the *Palaeolagus*, an early type of hare.

see from the illustration opposite which depicts a *Brontotherium platyceras*, a member of the group of Titanotheridae.

In its day, this was a very important group of animals, as large herds roamed the plains of North America.

In those days the plains had many pools and lakes where these beasts were able to find the soft juicy plants on which they thrived. Like the *Arsinotherium*, the horns with which they were equipped were bony outgrowths covered in skin.

Despite the success of the group as a whole, they remained surprisingly primitive, with small brains and awkward legs which must have resulted in an ungainly stride.

The *Brontotherium* was one of the largest members of the group, but this did not prevent it sharing the fate of all its other members when they died out about thirty-two million years ago.

There have been several suggestions as to why this very successful group died out, but most of them centre around the fact that the climate became a lot drier at this time. This in turn meant that the pools, where grew the soft plants that the *Brontotherium* ate, dried up.

Vast areas of grassland took their place. Grass is a very tough plant to eat and the large *Brontotherium* just did not have teeth strong enough to deal with the new food.

In the foreground of our illustration are three early hares, belonging to a species known as *Paleolagus*. Hares had originally evolved in Asia but soon spread over to America.

Though the increase in the grasslands spelt out death for the *Brontotherium*, it was the main cause of the development of large numbers of new animals which were adapted to life on the plains.

On the next pages you can see three of these creatures as well as the type of landscape where they would have lived.

On the right is a ferocious killer, by name *Dinictis felina*, which is chasing two of the new grass eaters, the *Hyracodon nebrasceinsis* in the centre, and the *Mesohippus bairdii* on the left which looks like a horse and indeed this is what it was, though it was only some sixty centimetres tall.

"*Mesohippus*" means "intermediate horse" and it was given this name because it was a very early example of a horse that lived out on the plains. The earlier horses had lived in forests.

Because it lived out on the open grassland, the *Mesohippus* needed to survive in a very different way from its ancestors which had lived in forests.

To begin with, it had to eat a different type of food, which the *Brontotherium* failed to do. In order to be able to eat the tough grasses instead of tree leaves, the teeth of the *Mesohippus* were not the same as those of its ancestors.

The grinding teeth, known as molars, grew much larger and more rugged, to break down the tough grass stems. But there is no doubt that it continued to eat the leaves of the bushes which were to be found scattered over the plains.

On these open plains it was useless for the *Mesohippus* to try to hide from hungry predators for the simple reason that there was nowhere to hide.

Its only chance of escape was to outrun the hunter. To this end the *Mesohippus*, through evolution, became faster than its ancestors had ever been.

Overleaf is a dramatic scene from millions of years ago. The hunter, *Dinictis*, is leaping at a *Hyracodon* while some *Mesohippus* escape.

It walked on its hooves instead of on the whole surface of the foot. Already the middle toe, which later became the only useful hoof, was the most important.

The leg bones were also adapting to a faster way of life. The *Mesohippus* could run and trot like the present-day horse.

Living at the same time was the *Hyracodon*, which was also a creature that grazed out on the open plains of North America. Though it may look similar to the *Mesohippus*, it was not a horse but a rhinoceros.

The gentle *Palaeomeryx* was one of the earliest deer. They did not have antlers but the males had long canine teeth.

them for survival, a contest that the *Hyracodons* were to lose.

They lost this contest and faded into extinction simply because the horses may have been more efficient at eating grass, and may also have been faster runners than the *Hyracodons*. They were thus better able to escape predators.

In the same picture you can see one of these killers. It is *Dinictis*, one of the earliest of the cats, which have been hunters of plant eaters down to the present day. Though it was only just over one metre in length, it must have taken a fearful toll of the wandering herds of small herbivores. It is from such a creature as the *Dinictis* that later big cats have descended.

It is important to note that a sudden change in climate might mean the end of one type of animal, but it can easily mean the chance for the evolution of another type of animal that otherwise may never have existed.

### Ancient Relatives of today's Mammals

In Europe about thirteen million years ago, there lived one of the earliest deer. It is called *Palaeomeryx kaupi* and was about the size of a small roe deer.

Unlike the present-day deer, it did not possess any antlers, a feature that deer did not gain until more recent times. But the adult male did have large canine teeth that were distinctly curved.

It most probably lived in damp marshy forests and its hooves were well adapted for this type of ground as they splayed out and helped to save the *Palaeomeryx* from sinking if it was unlucky enough to stray into a patch of deep mud.

Not only did the *Hyracodon* have a similar type of leg to that of the *Mesohippus* for running, it also developed the three toes of the latter animal.

These two families of mammals were trying to live in the same way as each other, so there was competition between

The curious shovel-shaped mouth of the *Platybelodon* was very useful for scooping up the water plants on which it lived.

The *Palaeomeryx* became extinct eleven million years ago but the evolution of the deer family went on to result in the mighty red deer of the Scottish glens and a whole host of others, some of which we will meet later in this book.

By eleven million years ago the elephant family (see page 16) had spread all over the world and had developed into many different species.

One of the most peculiar is pictured opposite. It is known as the *Platybelodon grangeri*, a member of the Mastodon group of elephants. It was probably the most grotesque mastodon ever to have lived. But that amazing mouth was very useful to the *Platybelodon*.

This mastodon lived around the edges of lakes and along rivers, which gives us a clue to the use it made of its strange lower jaw. This jaw was not only unusually long but it was also very wide. There can be little doubt that the *Platybelodon* used it as a shovel to uproot food from the mud near the lakes and rivers.

The jaw was finished off with a pair of flat incisors which were strong and shaped something like chisels.

It is easy to imagine this creature as it wandered along the shores of some ancient lake, scooping up large amounts of water plants to satisfy its appetite.

Because of its particular method of feeding it did not really need a trunk, like other elephants, to grasp food, because its jaw did this job most effectively.

So the trunk was only to be seen as a thick muscular lip that projected down to the end of the lower jaw and was probably used to move food from the digging front teeth to the back of the mouth ready to be swallowed.

Though this was a member of the elephant family, it may be surprising to learn that it stood a mere one and two thirds metres tall, much smaller than the modern elephant.

Despite this, the skull of the *Platybelodon* was one and three quarters of a metre long, so that the skull was longer than the animal was tall. This was a most unusual development but a useful one, for it enabled this mastodon to dig up its food without having to stoop.

While the *Platybelodon* was living out its life wading in the shallows of lakes in Asia, there were two quite different animals living on the dry plains of North America. These two mammals are shown on the next two pages.

On the left is an animal that looked rather like a modern giraffe. This is an *Alticamelus latus* and was in fact a member of the camel family.

It may be surprising to find a camel in America for we usually think of them as coming from Arabia. But ten million years ago the world was a very different place and the camels were then a particularly widespread group.

The *Alticamelus* was about three and one half metres tall. There can be little doubt that it used its height to reach the leaves and young shoots that were to be found high up in the trees.

During evolution the bones in the neck had grown longer but without increasing in number which meant that this long neck, so useful for reaching high leaves, was not very manoevrable.

The same is true of the legs, where the individual bones had increased in length, producing the long, stilt-like legs.

It is possible that, like today's giraffes, they were not herd animals but moved around singly or in groups of just a few animals.

This singular animal was very successful in its way of life, probably because there was so little competition for the food that it ate. As a species it survived for about nine million years, and died out about five million years ago.

The *Alticamelus* was not the only unusual camel at this time, for the camels evolved into several highly specialised types, including one, the *Stenomylus* that looked more like a modern gazelle.

As the *Alticamelus* evolved into a tall animal it would be safe to assume that another creature evolving in such a way as to suit the same way of life would be similar in appearance. This was so. For

example, the modern giraffe looks rather like the *Alticamelus*, though it is not related. This is known as convergence.

Living out on the same plains along with the *Alticamelus* was a very different animal, the *Merychippus primus*.

As you can see from the picture above it was a horse. It marked the next stage in

The giraffe-like camel, *Alticamelus*, watches as a group of *Merychippus* flee from the wildfire in this scene from ten million years ago.

the evolution of the horse, after the *Mesohippus* had moved out on to the plains many millions of years previously (see illustration page 24).

However, it should not be thought that the evolutionary trail of the horse led from the *Mesohippus* to the *Merychippus* and so on to the present-day horse. In fact these different stages of horse just represent the stages that horse evolution has gone through and do not necessarily relate to the true ancestors of the horse.

The *Merychippus* was only about the size of a modern donkey but it was far more horse-like than the *Mesohippus*, which had only just taken to a life on the plains.

The legs of this horse were well adapted for running, so if a hungry predator threatened a herd of these creatures, they could have used their legs to race across the plains, leaving the hunter worn out and hungrier than ever.

Perhaps the only chance that such a predator would have had of snatching a *Merychippus* would have been if it could single out an old or ill member of the herd that could not run as fast as the rest.

Though the leg of the *Merychippus* was very horse-like the hoof on the end of it still had three toes, just as the earlier horses had. But the centre toe was much larger than the two outer toes. Indeed these outer toes could not even touch the ground and the animal only walked on the middle one.

This stage in horse evolution was very important for it was soon after the time of the *Merychippus* that the two great horse branches separated. One branch lost the outer toes altogether. This made for faster galloping.

It was this group that gave rise to the present-day horses and zebras. The other group, known as Hipparions, kept the outer toes but became specialised in trotting.

For many millions of years the Hipparions were just as important as the true horses but they eventually became extinct a few million years ago.

Before we leave the *Merychippus* it is worth remarking that it was a true grazer living solely on grass, unlike the *Mesohippus* that fed on the leaves of bushes as well. Its teeth were very tough and heavily ridged in order to deal with the completely grass diet.

It is from fossils that we can see how the teeth of the forest-living ancestor became tough enough to cope with the new food – grass – and how the legs developed to allow the horses to run faster and enable them to escape the meat

The graceful *Dicrocerus* lived in Europe about seven million years ago. It was the first deer to possess antlers.

eaters that preyed on them. Thus, finally, the horse that we know today evolved.

A few million years after the *Palaeomeryx* (see page 27) there lived another early species of deer. It is named *Dicrocerus elegans* and it lived about seven million years ago. It is pictured on pages 32 and 33.

This deer was the first to grow antlers, though they were still primitive and simple compared to the magnificent antlers of later species of deer.

The true deer came from Asia and though the *Dicrocerus* lived in Europe, it

The walrus-like *Desmostylus* lived some eight million years ago. It is thought that it may be related to the Manatee family.

undoubtedly had relatives in the East.

Like many modern deer it lived in forests that in those days stretched over far more of Europe than today. The *Dicrocerus* itself became extinct, but it was not long before the deer family grew to include many types, with different antlers, including the red deer of today.

At the beginning of this book (page 4) you can see an animal that at first sight may be taken for a deer. This is the *Synthetoceras*. But appearances can be deceptive especially in the field of palaeontology, for it belongs to the North American group of mammals known as Pronghorns.

Today there is only one species of pronghorn left, but millions of years ago they were one of the most important groups of animals in North America.

There were many different species and each sported a different growth on the head. But these were not antlers. They were horns. Modern deer shed their antlers each year and grow new, larger ones in the next spring. However, creatures such as pronghorns and cattle keep their headgear all the time and they grow larger as the animals grow older.

On page 12 of this book you can see how one family of mammals took to the water. This was the Siren family and their descendants are still to be seen in quiet coastal waters.

Other animals, though, were taking to the water and you can see one of these, pictured opposite.

It is the *Desmostylus* which lived near and on the coasts of the Northern Pacific a few million years ago.

This creature was a member of the Desmostylan family which, it is thought, may be related to the Siren and Elephant families. But there is some doubt about this as the fossils of early Desmostylans have never been found in Africa where the fossils of sirens and elephants *have* been found.

The *Desmostylus* had a rather large head for its size and some very impressive teeth that jutted out from its mouth, giving an appearance rather similar to that of a modern walrus.

It may have used these teeth to prise shellfish off the rocks to which they were clinging and then used its strong back teeth to crack open the hard shell and reach the juicy meal inside.

The whole group of Desmostylans became extinct about seven million years ago, perhaps as a result of the seal family taking over their source of food. Both groups were very well adapted to life in the water by virtue of a streamlined body and flippers.

These seals seem to have evolved from the same family group as dogs.

### The Sabre-toothed Tiger

Five million years ago in Europe there lived what is perhaps the best-known of all prehistoric mammals, the mighty Sabre-toothed Tiger.

In fact, there were many different types of sabre-toothed animals and none of them was a tiger. To understand this we must go back to the time of the *Dinictis* (page 24.) From such a creature two branches of the cat family evolved. One we know today, for all present-day cats belong to it. The other is called Machairodontidae which was a hunter of large animals on the plains.

On the next two pages you can see a member of the horse family, the *Hipparion mediterraneum* confronted by a *Machairodus cultridens*, one of the largest of the sabre-toothed cats. It was about the same size as a modern tiger.

Like all the sabre-toothed cats, the *Machairodus* had enormous canine teeth.

These great teeth had evolved over the years as a highly successful way of killing prey.

Let us follow for a few moments, in our mind's eye, a *Machairodus* on a hunting expedition. Like most cats it probably hunted by stealth, using its padded feet and cunning to creep up as close as possible to its intended victim, possibly through long grass or hidden in bushes. It was at this point that those fearsome teeth would come into their own, for with one bound the great cat would be on its victim and use its powerful neck muscles to drive the canines home like two swords.

The dreadful wound thus inflicted would be enough to bring down the unfortunate creature and another meal would lie at the feet of the hungry *Machairodus*.

In order to use its deadly canines the cat had a lower jaw that could open more than ninety degrees and this allowed the sabre teeth an unimpeded strike at the intended victim.

The *Machairodus* lived out on the open grasslands and its prey must have consisted mainly of the larger hoofed animals that roamed the plain. The huge teeth were specially designed to deal with those large creatures.

An interesting point about the *Machairodus* is that, as the canines grew longer and longer, the other teeth became smaller and smaller so that by the time the *Machairodus* had fully evolved it was almost unable to chew its food.

This meant that it was only able to eat the really soft parts of a victim and had to leave most of its kill for scavengers to eat.

Since the big cat could only eat such a small part of its prey the hunt was only worth while if the intended quarry was a large animal.

The *Machairodus* had to kill a large number of these to survive. As a result the sabre-tooths depended on the vast herds of large herbivores that roamed the plains and when these great herds began to decrease the sabre-toothed cats were doomed to extinction.

Though the *Machairodus* and all its relatives have long been extinct, they

The mighty *Machairodus*, or sabre-toothed tiger, hunted large animals, such as the *Hipparion*, in Europe five million years ago.

live on in man's imagination as one of the most ferocious killers ever known.

The creature that the *Machairodus* has surprised in our illustration is a *Hipparion mediterraneum*.

As its name suggests, it was a member of the very successful group of horses, known as the Hipparion, that spread from America to Europe about six million years ago by crossing the land bridge then spanning the Bering Straits.

Though they were very successful on the grasslands of Southern Europe, they became extinct just a few million years ago, leaving the single-toed horse as the only surviving member of the horse family. Of course, this is the horse that we know today.

In the forests of Europe at this time there lived the huge beast that is pictured opposite. It is known as the *Deinotherium giganteum*. It was a member of the elephant family but it belonged to a group that has long been extinct.

The *Deinotherium* had very unusual downward pointing tusks that grew from its lower jaws and it had no upper tusks at all. It is thought that this three metre tall animal lived in damp forests and ate the leaves off the trees. The use to which it put its curious tusks is not known but it has been suggested that they were useful for digging up roots.

How this tall elephant evolved is not really clear. We know from fossils that there was a whole group of similar animals but all the fossils are of creatures already with the characteristic long legs and down-turned tusks. There are no early examples showing the development of these features.

The *Deinotherium* lived in Europe and became extinct about two million years ago, just as so many other groups of elephants were to die out before the present day.

### In the Southern Hemisphere

On the page overleaf and on several following pages we shall be examining the creatures that lived in South America long ago and are now all extinct.

The story of the mammals of South America is very interesting because they evolved entirely separately from the rest of the world until about three million years ago, when a great disaster overtook them. To begin the story of the mammals of South America we must go back to the *Deltatheridium* (page 8.)

In those far-off days the continents of Africa, Australia, Antarctica and South America were joined together into one vast continent which we refer to today as Gondwanaland.

Then, by the process known as Continental Drift, Africa moved to the north to meet the Northern Continent made up of Eurasia and North America.

Soon after Africa moved to the North, the group of mammals known as Marsupials evolved in Gondwanaland and spread all over it. Marsupials are mammals that carry their young in pouches.

Then at about the end of the reign of the Dinosaurs, Australia broke away and Antarctica began to freeze over, killing off all its life.

This left South America alone. Meanwhile in the Northern Continent, the mammals known as Placentals (that do not have pouches) had developed.

Somehow it is thought that some very primitive Placentals reached South America, but after this, South America was isolated from the rest of the world for over fifty million years.

The huge *Deinotherium* belonged to an extinct family of elephants. It is not known for what purpose it used its curious tusks.

Most of this is just theory but it does seem to fit the facts of what happened many years ago.

During the millions of years when South America was a separate continent, it developed a unique animal life. The Placentals evolved into two groups of plant eaters, while the Marsupials evolved almost exclusively into meat eaters.

Opposite are two of the herbivores that once lived in this isolated continent. They are the *Toxodon* and the *Pyrotherium*.

The *Toxodon* looked very much like a modern rhinoceros, but was unrelated. It was, in fact, the last of a long line of creatures known as Toxodonts.

The Toxodont line was already thirty million years old by the time the *Toxodon* appeared.

It was the scientist Charles Darwin who first discovered a fossil of this massively built animal. It was the fossilised skull of a *Toxodon* and it was being used as a target in a stone-throwing contest by some South American farm boys.

The other creature in our picture is known today as a *Pyrotherium*. This huge animal was all of four metres long and resembled a modern elephant. Not only did it have a trunk and teeth that were enlarged so as to be almost tusks but the other teeth were very much like those of early elephants to be found in Egypt.

As time went by the process of continental drift took South America further and further north until, about three million years ago, the Isthmus of Panama was formed, making a land bridge from North America to the Southern Continent, spelling out extinction for most of the animals in South America.

When this land bridge was first formed animals from North America travelled south in search of food and some from South America went north for the same reason. However, in the fight for survival, it was mainly the creatures from the north that survived because they were so much better at obtaining food.

Let us look at three of the animals that lived in South America when the link was formed with North America and see how they fared in the face of competition from the more advanced mammals of the north.

Each of these three beasts can be seen on pages 42 and 43. The first, known as *Macrauchenia*, had a very strange appearance. It was built something like a camel, though of course it was unrelated. But it had a short trunk which it used to pluck the vegetation on which it fed. This odd creature (its name means "large throat") became extinct when the more advanced mammals from the north robbed it of its food by eating it themselves.

The second animal is the *Thylacosmilus atrox*, one of the many marsupial hunters that roamed South America before the placental carnivores arrived from the north. This beast was one and a third metres long and was the largest marsupial carnivore yet known. Like the sabre-toothed cats of the northern continents, the *Thylacosmilus* had huge canine teeth that it used to stab its prey and strong neck muscles to drive home those deadly fangs.

Unlike the sabre-toothed tigers, however, the *Thylacosmilus* still had the rest of its teeth and so was able to chew its food. Despite this, it could not compete with the invasion of the carnivores from North America, and it passed into extinction soon after the moving together

The bulky *Toxodon* was the last in a long line of Toxodonts. The *Pyrotherium* may have had a trunk but it was not related to the elephant.

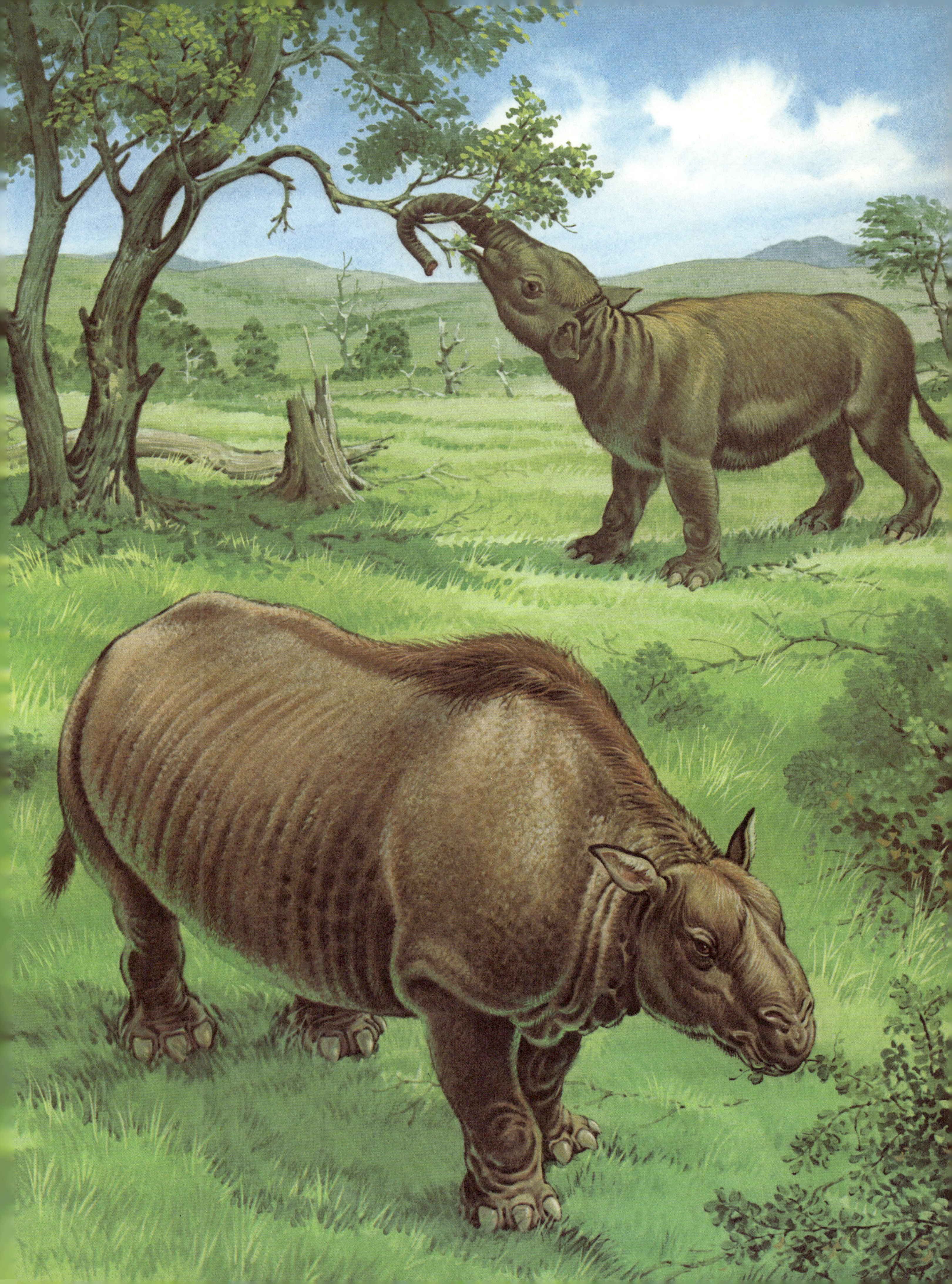

of the two continents. But not all the mammals of South America died out. The opossum, for example, spread to North America and now lives extensively over both continents.

The third animal in the picture above is an armadillo. The armadillos were the only group of mammals to have evolved a bony covering for their bodies. Turtles and other reptiles have retained their bony armour from earlier times but the armadillos had to evolve it, for the ancestral armadillo, the *Metacheiomys*, had no armour at all. In most of the armadillos the armour is jointed so that the animal can curl up into a ball when danger threatens. But the *Glyptodon*, which was a huge member of the group of armadillos, (it was two and a half metres long, not including its long armoured tail) had a solid dome of armour, more like a tortoise. When the two Americas joined together the *Glyptodon* was more successful than most, for it survived the invasion from the north. Indeed, it did not become extinct until about one million years ago and its smaller relatives are still to be found in the old hunting grounds of the *Glyptodon*.

## Prehistoric Animals of Australia

When Gondwanaland was breaking up, Australia broke away before the early Placentals reached South America, the result being that there were only marsupials living in Australia, a situation that remained until man imported sheep and

The cat-like *Thylacosmilus*, the camel-like *Macrauchenia* and the armadillo lived about three million years ago.

other animals. Some of the Australian marsupials that lived there a million years ago are shown on the next two pages.

During what is known as the Pleistocene Age, the animals in Australia grew to be larger than they are today.

The largest marsupial known was the *Diprotodon*, on the left of the picture on page 45. The *Diprotodon* was a member of the wombat family.

Many fossils of this animal have been found preserved in mud that was then at the bottom of lakes. Since the *Diprotodon* was not a water creature, how did the fossils get there? What may have happened was this.

During a long hot summer all those years ago, the shallow lakes – and there were several – may have dried up and the top of the mud baked dry to form a thin crust on which plants could grow and small animals walk. If a huge *Diprotodon* tried to walk on the surface of baked mud to reach a tasty plant, its enormous weight would have been too heavy for the crust which would have given way, plunging the unfortunate *Diprotodon* into the almost liquid mud below the crust. The *Diprotodon* would then have been trapped and its fossil preserved in the mud for modern scientists later to discover. Just such an incident is shown in the picture.

The wombats are not the only animals to have had giant relatives alive a million years ago. There was then a large species of kangaroo bounding across the land.

This animal, known today as *Procoptodon*, was a good three metres tall, nearly twice the size of modern kangaroos. It lived in probably the same way as kangaroos today for it moved in groups that ranged over the grasslands and ate the grass and bushes growing there.

The third of the Australian Marsupials shown in the picture above is the *Thylacinus*, or Tasmanian Wolf. This dog-sized hunter may still roam remote areas of Tasmania but it is thought to be extinct. A million years ago, though, it was common in Australia and about half as large again as the modern animal.

Though it may not have been able to run very fast, it had great powers of endurance and could still be running when the creature it was hunting dropped from exhaustion.

It is not only marsupials that have managed to survive in Australasia. The world's only Monotremes live there, too. These are very primitive mammals which lay eggs. The well-known duck-billed platypus is a Monotreme.

### The Mighty Mastodon

About two hundred thousand years ago, North America was inhabited by one of the last members of a once very successful group of elephants, the Mastodons. At one time, Mastodons were to be found in Europe, but by the beginning of the Pleistocene Age, two million years ago, they had all died out in Europe. Only the *Mastodon americanus* was left and this species was to become extinct about ten thousand years ago. The *Mastodon americanus* first evolved about three hundred thousand years ago and ranged over the whole of North America.

Because it was such a common animal, there were many fossils of its bones preserved all over America. There is scarcely a natural history museum in America that does not have the remains of one of these giants somewhere amongst its fossil collection.

When it was alive this *Mastodon* stood about three metres tall at the shoulder, so it would compare well with a modern elephant so far as size goes. Like most Mastodons of this group, its teeth had high ridges and deep ruts which resulted in a strong grinding tooth. The tusks of this beast reveal at a glance whether the fossil bones belonged to a male or a female *Mastodon*. The male had both upper and lower tusks, though the lower ones were only about eighteen centimetres long. On the other hand, the females did not have lower tusks at all and their upper tusks were not as long, nor as curved, as those of a male.

A *Diprotodon* has become trapped in the mud. A *Thylacinus* watches hungrily and a group of *Procoptodons* bound away in the distance.

Perhaps the reason why this particular *Mastodon* survived so long is that it had a coat of long hair that would have kept it warm during the Ice Ages, whilst other *Mastodons* did not have this coat.

Many skeletons of this *Mastodon* have been found in the famous tar-pits of California. These have now solidified into rock so that the fossils in them can be removed. But eleven thousand years

A *Mastodon* trapped in a tar-pit in Western America, is about to be attacked by wolf-like carnivores.

ago, tar-pits were death traps. Because water will not seep through tar, any rain that fell would naturally have lain in pools on the surface of the tar. If any *Mastodon* passing needed a drink of water, it may well have walked on to the tar to reach the water. In doing so, it would have become stuck, and the more it struggled, the deeper it sank. Faced with such a target, the hunters of the area would have quickly gathered to take advantage of such an easy prey. In trying to reach the *Mastodon*, though, they would have been trapped themselves. This is probably why there are so many more meat eaters found in the tar-pits than plant eaters. Our illustration above depicts a trapped Mastodon at bay.

When the *Mastodon americanus* died out about ten thousand years ago, it may have been the end of the Mastodons, but it was not the end of elephant life in the two Americas, for some scientists have put forward the suggestion that the Imperial Mammoth, *Mammuthus imperator*, (shown on page 6) may have survived until only two thousand years ago in South America.

## The Ice Ages

The last two million years or so have been marked by Ice Ages, each lasting up to two hundred thousand years. The most recent ended eleven thousand years ago. These cold periods were separated by warmer periods. Much of the land was covered by great sheets of ice. Around the edges of the ice sheets lay vast treeless plains that suffered bitterly cold winters but had a lot of plant life in the warmer months. The animals that lived there had to adapt to the new climate. One such animal was the *Elasmotherium sibricum* (seen below) which lived on the plains of South-western

The huge *Elasmotherium* lived in Europe just two hundred thousand years ago. Its horn was a massive two metres long.

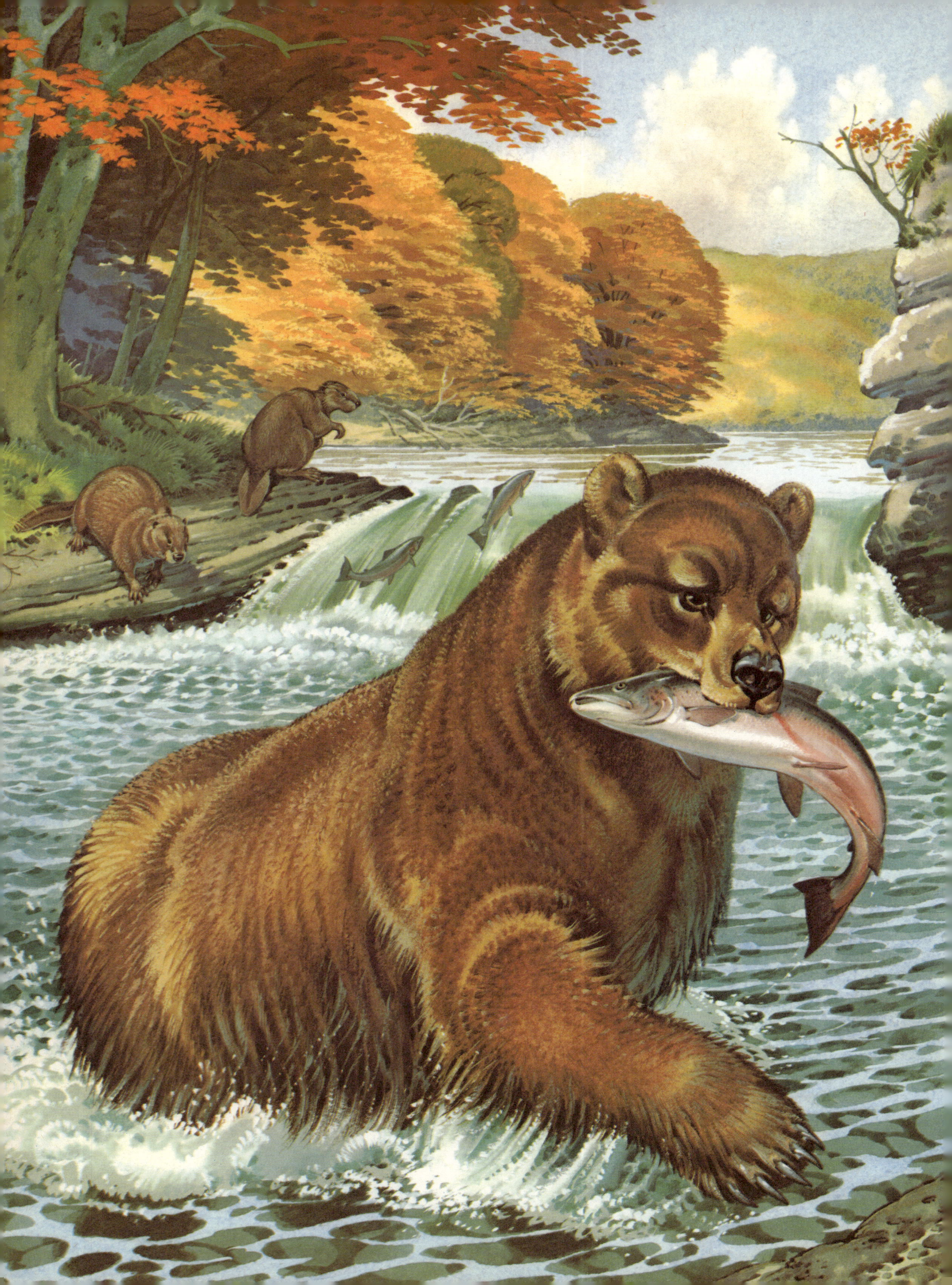

The Cave Bear or *Ursus spelaeus*, larger than today's Brown bear, lived in much the same way. The *Trogontherium* was a giant beaver.

Europe about two hundred thousand years ago. Unlike the *Hyracodon* (page 24) and the *Indricotherium* (page 20) it was of the classic rhinoceros shape, complete with horn. Indeed, it *was* a rhinoceros. Earlier rhinos from Asia had slowly spread into Europe and on the way had become adapted to living out on the open plains. The *Elasmotherium* was the high point of this evolution but when it died out it left no descendants.

It is possible that the advance of the ice took away the *Elasmotherium*'s habitat of open grasslands. Since it was so specialised for life on the plains, it is probable that the *Elasmotherium* could not adapt to a new way of life, unlike its relative, the Woolly Rhinoceros (see page 55.)

However in its day it must have been an imposing sight as it strode the plains, for it was no less than twice the size of the modern black rhinoceros. The horn on its head would surely have been enough to daunt any predator which thought of the *Elasmotherium* as a future meal. That horn was anything up to two metres long, the largest horn of any rhinoceros that we know of today.

Opposite is a picture of the Cave Bear, or *Ursus spelaeus*. It is known as the Cave Bear for the simple reason that it spent its winters hibernating in the shelter of caves. As a result many fossils have been found buried in cave floors. One cave was found to have as many as thirty thousand bear fossils lying in it. These are the remains of bears which had died from natural causes during winter hibernation in the caves over thousands of years.

The *Ursus spelaeus* lived in deciduous forests in most of Europe and South-west Asia. It ate a diet that seems to have been mainly made up of plants, for the fossilised teeth are very worn as a result of eating too much tough plant food.

However, like modern bears, the *Ursus spelaeus* probably ate fish and other small creatures if it could catch them. This large bear – it was about the size of a modern grizzly bear – became extinct about twenty thousand years ago when the northern forests where it dwelt diminished in size.

In the background of the picture can be seen something that is familiar in North America to this day. It is a dam built by beavers across a river to form a small lake behind it. But the beavers which built the dam in our illustration were nearly three metres long, over twice the size of modern beavers. These giant beavers are known to scientists as *Trogontherium*.

On the following pages you can see a confrontation that may have taken place any time between three hundred thousand and twelve thousand years ago in Europe, for that is the period when both these animals were alive. They are now extinct.

The large deer has been named *Megaloceros giganteus* but it is more often called the Irish Elk, even though it was not an elk and did not only live in Ireland. It received this inaccurate name, because its remains were discovered in large numbers in the peat bogs of Ireland.

Since it was so large and because its antlers resembled those of an elk in some ways, it was thought to be an extinct type of that animal. Hence the name Irish Elk. Its antlers could be nearly four metres across.

The antlers (up to four metres across) of the *Megaloceros* or Irish Elk, see overleaf, must have daunted even the *Panthera spelaeus*.

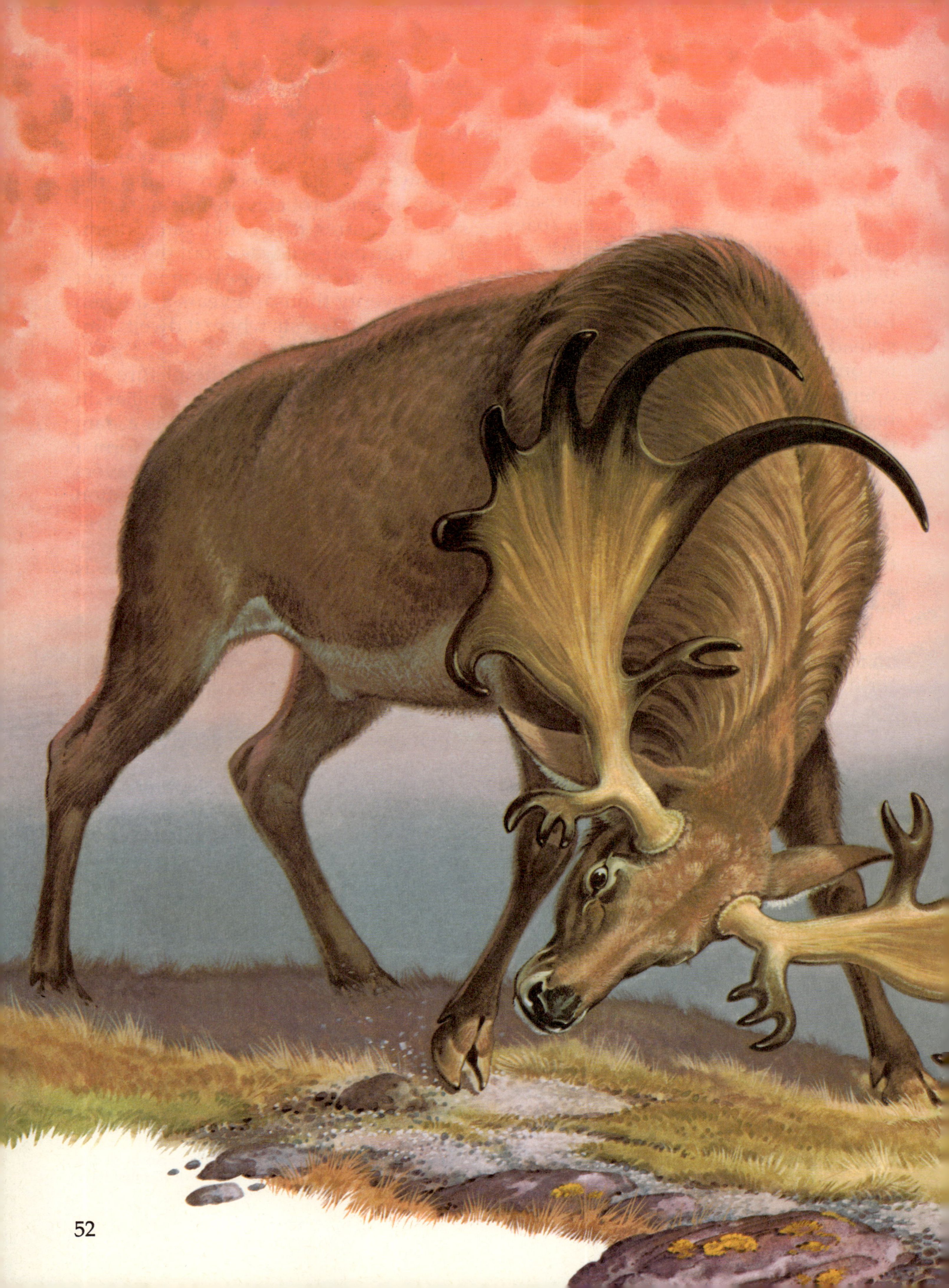

53

A form of this deer had evolved in the forests some time before, and over the years the creature evolved larger and larger, in particular its antlers. These seem to have developed more quickly than the body of the deer, so the animal became almost top heavy.

The size of the antlers must have made life in the forest almost impossible, as the antlers would have become entangled in the branches of trees. So it is not surprising that the Irish Elk took to life on the open plains.

It is probable that the Irish Elk did not live in herds, but singly. There were many of these magnificent animals living up to twelve thousand years ago, when they became extinct. This was probably due to two causes, the first being the reduction of their natural habitat, at the end of the last Ice Age. The second cause was man who must have seen in the Irish Elk a good source of food and may have hunted it to extinction.

The large cat that is threatening the Irish Elk in the picture is the Cave Lion, more properly called *Panthera spelaea*. This cat was the largest in Europe at this time. Indeed it was a good deal larger than the present-day African lion. It had an extremely thick coat which helped to stave off the rigours of the northern winters.

The *Panthera* measured in length about two metres and was possibly lightly striped. It earned its name of Cave Lion because some of its fossils were discovered in a cave.

## The Woolly Mammals

In order to survive in the bitter cold of an Ice Age, an animal had to change to suit the new climate. One creature which managed to do this very well is pictured opposite. It is the Woolly Rhinoceros or

In the bitter cold of the Ice Ages only a well-adapted animal like the Woolly Rhinoceros could survive.

*Coelodonta antiquitatis* to use its scientific name.

This well-known beast was very common in Europe between four hundred thousand and twenty-five thousand years ago. As the weather got colder, it became adapted to the climate with the help of its famous woolly coat. The long coarse outer layer would have been a protection against the biting winds and rain and snow. Under this outer layer there was an inner layer of soft fluffy fur that must have kept the animal very warm indeed. Protected by such a coat, the Woolly Rhinoceros could probably have put up with such bad weather as you can see in the picture.

As the climate grew colder the rhinoceros found that there was much less food around. What little food there was could not support great numbers of large animals and the rhinoceros developed into a much smaller animal. It then did not need as much food to keep going.

The Woolly Rhinoceros lived on the steppes that covered most of Europe during the Ice Ages and fed on the grass that grew there. It is probable that when winter struck and the grassland furthest north became uninhabitable, the rhinoceros migrated south for the winter, before returning north in the spring.

On the next two pages is a splendid illustration of what is surely the most famous of all the prehistoric animals, the Woolly Mammoth. Like the Woolly Rhinoceros, the Woolly Mammoth was adapted to the bitter cold of the times.

*Mammuthus* (overleaf) was the well-known Woolly Mammoth that survived in the Ice Ages because of its long shaggy coat.

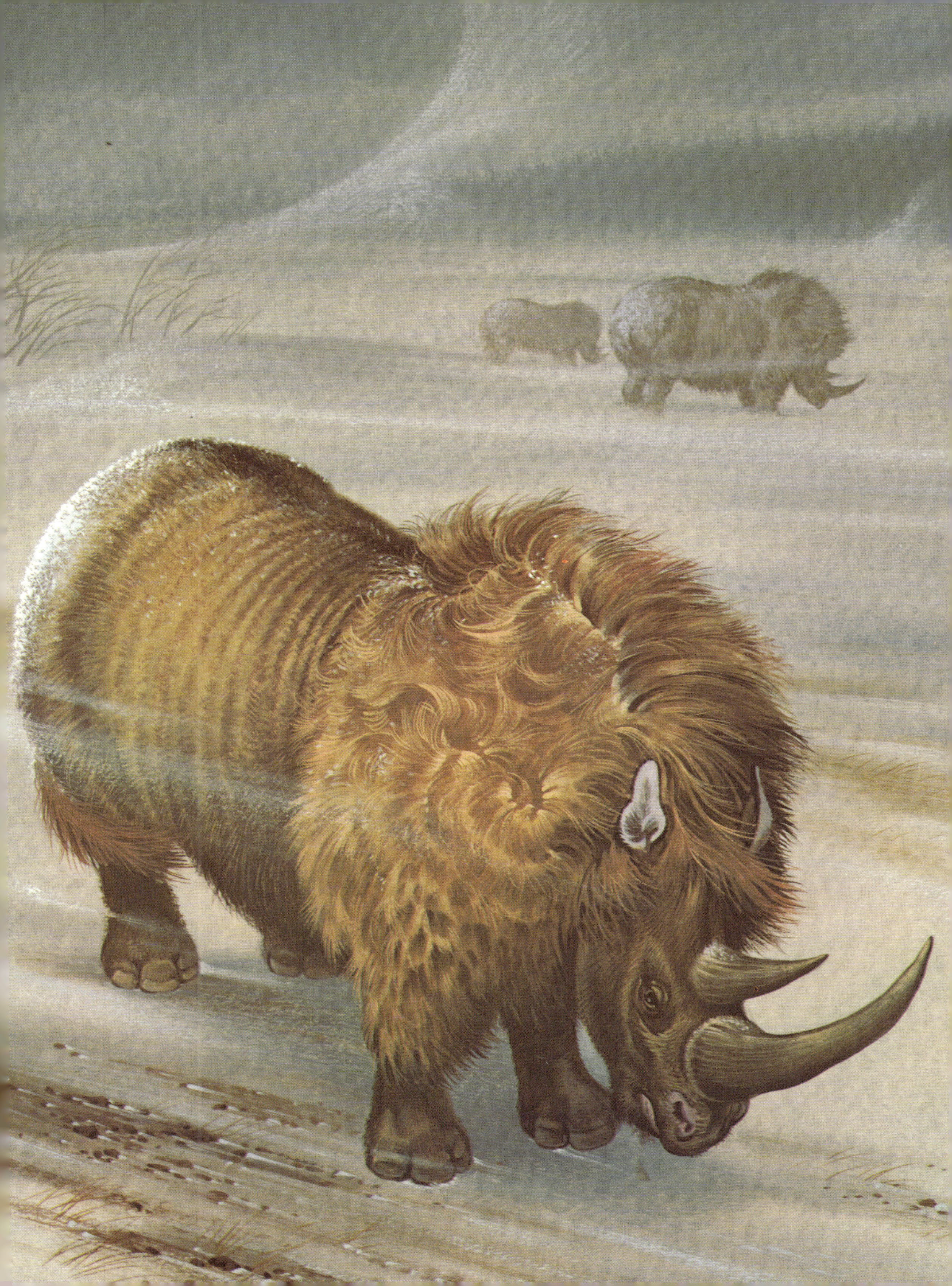

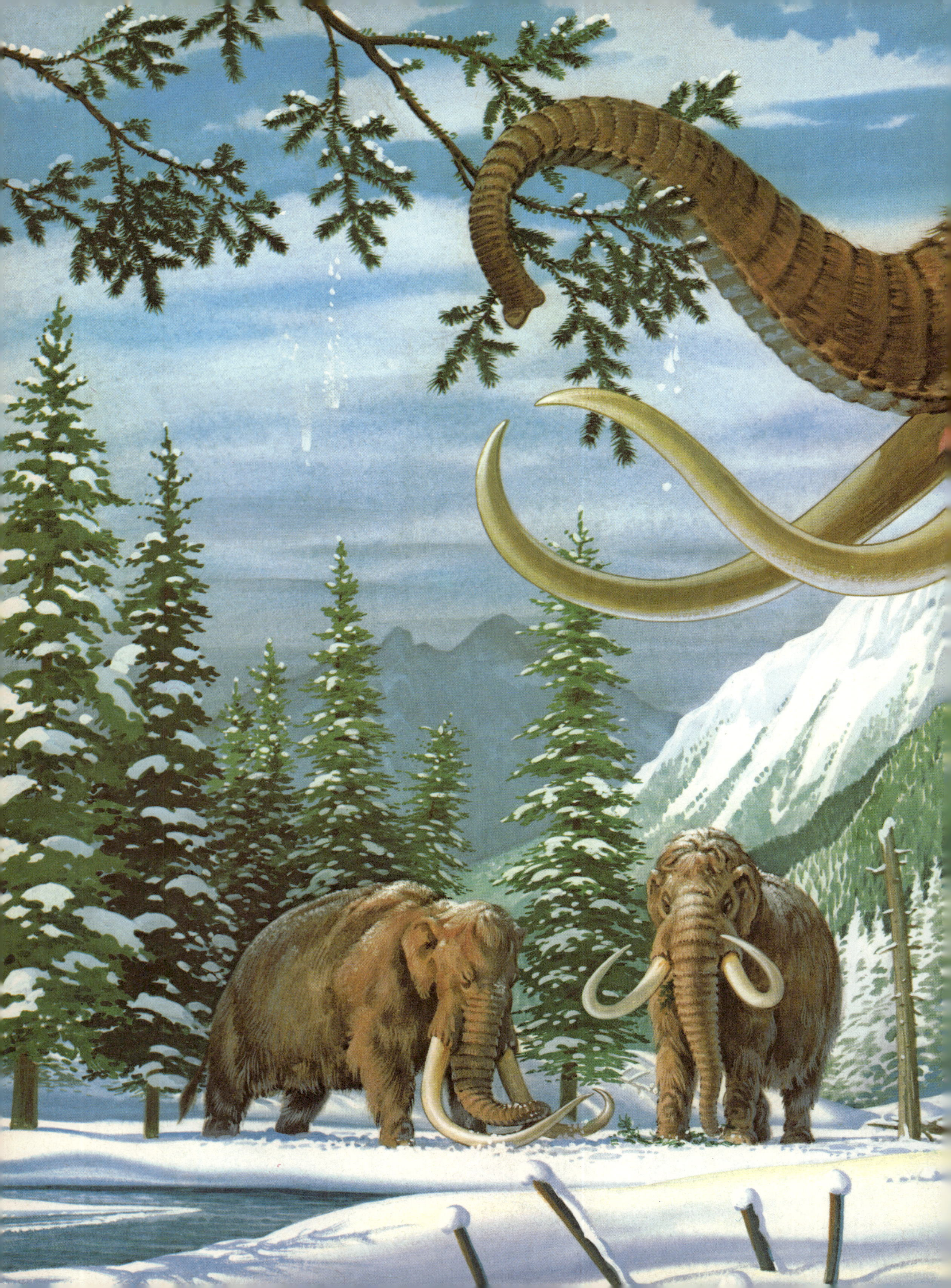

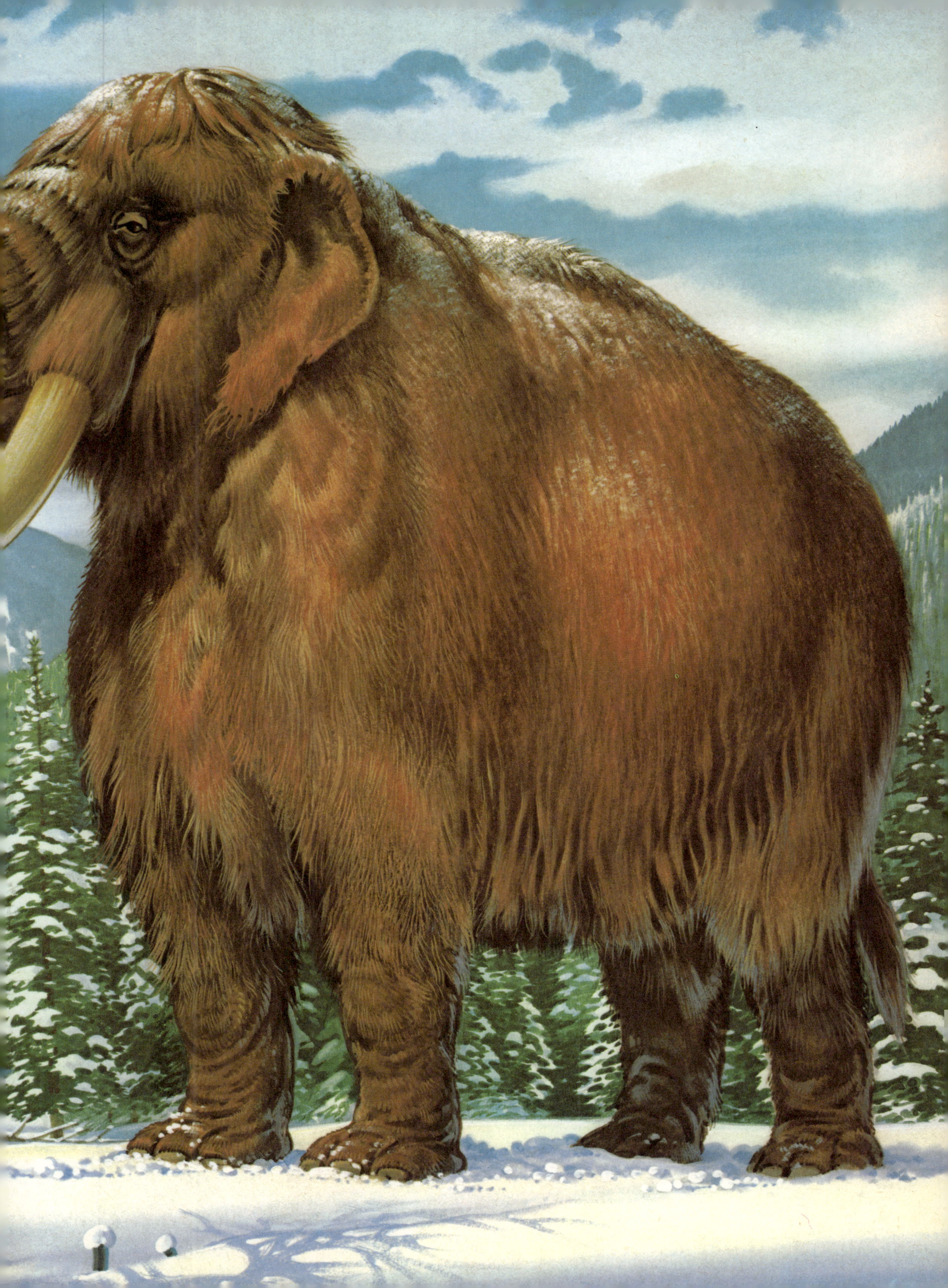

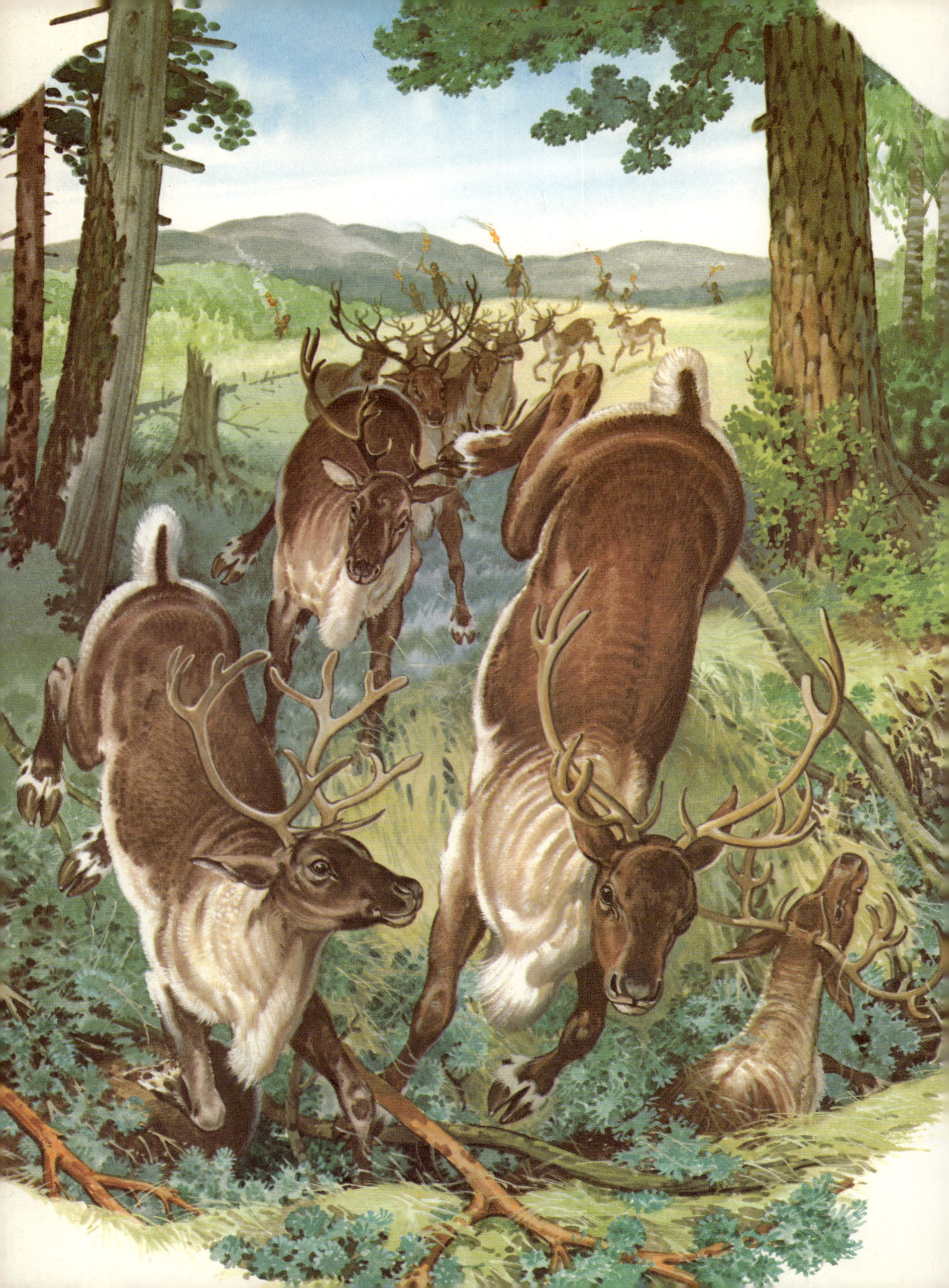

The arrival of man, the greatest hunter of all, affected the wild life in many ways. Not least was his hunting of many creatures.

The shaggy coat was similar to that of the Woolly Rhinoceros. It had two layers of hair to keep the animal warm. Like the Rhinoceros again, the Woolly Mammoth (today called *Mammuthus primigenius*) grew smaller during the Ice Ages. It was about three metres tall compared to the height reached by the Imperial Mammoth (page 6.)

Most of the other creatures in this book we only know about because their fossil bones have been discovered. However there are remains of the Woolly Mammoth which scientists are able to study, complete with all the muscles and other soft parts of the body. There are no mammoths alive today, of course, but in the frozen wastes of Siberia a number of mammoth bodies have been found. They had been preserved as if in a deep freeze during the years since they died. From studying these remains we can even tell what the mammoths ate just before they died. In their stomachs have been found leaves and shoots from willows, fir trees and many types of bush.

When the ice sheets retreated about eleven thousand years ago, the Woolly Mammoth retreated north with them. Eventually the number of mammoths and rhinoceroses fell, and it may have been the hunting carried out by prehistoric man that finished off the last survivors of these giants of the Ice Ages.

Not all the Ice Age animals died out, however. The musk ox (*Moschus*) and the polar bear, for example, both lived alongside the mammoth and both still roam the Arctic north today.

The Woolly Mammoth had huge curved tusks which became larger and more curved as the beast grew older. These large tusks could possibly have been useful in clearing the ground of snow if the mammoth could not get at the food it needed.

When fossils of this creature were first found, it was thought to be a primitive form of elephant. This is how it received its first name, *Elephus primigenius* which means first-born elephant. As we have seen, however, it was really a very advanced species of elephant and was named *Mammuthus primigenius*. The true early elephants had existed many millions of years previously.

In the period of time between the end of the last Ice Age and the present day there have been a large number of extinctions.

To some extent these may have been due to the change in climate, but there can be little doubt that many of the larger animals were hunted into extinction by man or lost their feeding grounds to man's agriculture.

Today in Europe and North America there are few large animals left in the wild.

But not all the large mammals were killed off by man. Some were first hunted, later domesticated and kept by man in herds to provide a constant source of food.

On the opposite page some early hunters are hunting reindeer by driving them towards a pit.

Once in such a pit, reindeer would have been easily slain with the spears and other weapons that early man possessed. However, some animals (including the reindeer) are now domesticated and kept by man to provide meat.

With the appearance of man we reach our own times, having seen many of the animals that have played a part in the development of the Earth into the world we see around us today.

# Pronunciations

**Alticamelus latus** –
Al-tee-CAM-elus LAH-tuss

**Andrewsarchus mongoliensis** –
An-droo-SAR-kuss mon-goh-lee-EN-siss

**Arsinotherium zitteli** –
Ah-sin-oh-THEE-ree-um zit-TELL-ee

**Brontotherium platyceras** –
Bron-toe-THEE-ree-um platt-ISS-eras

**Casteroides** –
Caster-OY-dees

**Coelondonta antiquitatis** –
SEEL-oh-DON-ta anti-quee-TART-iss

**Condylarthra** –
Con-dee-LAR-thrah

**Creodont** –
CREE-oh-dohnt

**Deinotherium giganteum** –
DYN-oh-THEE-ree-um jy-GAN-tee-um

**Deltatheridium** –
Dell-ta-the RID-ee-um

**Desmostylus** –
Desmoh-STY-luss

**Dicrocerus elegans** –
DY-cross-erus ELL-ee-gans

**Dinictis felina** –
Dy-NICK-tiss fee-LIE-nah

**Diptrodon** –
DIP-trow-don

**Elasmotherium sibricum** –
Ee-LAZ-moh-THEE-ree-um SYB-ree-cum

**Eocene** –
EE-oh-seen

**Glyptodon** –
GLIP-toe-don

**Hipparion Mediterraneum** –
Hip-AH-ree-on med-it-er-RAIN-ee-um

**Hyracodon nebrasceinsis** –
High-RACK-oh-DON nee-brah-SKIN-siss

**Icaronycteris** –
I-car-oh-NICK-ter-iss

**Indricotherium parvum** –
Inn-dree-coh-THEE-ree-um PAR-vum

**Machairodontidae** –
Mak-EER-roh-DON-tid-ee

**Machairodus cultridens** –
Mak-EER-ROH-duss cull-TRY-dens

**Macrauchenia** –
Mak-ROW-KEEN-ee-ah

**Mammuthus primigenius** –
Mamma-THUS pry-mee-GEE-nee-us

**Mastodon americanus** –
MASS-toe-DON am-erry-CARN-us

**Megalocerus giganteus** –
Megga-LOSS-eruss jy-GANT-ee-uss

**Merychippus primus** –
Merry-KIP-uss PRY-muss

**Mesohippus** –
Meez-oh-HIPP-uss

**Metacheiomys** –
Met-ack-EE-oh-miss

**Miacid** –
My-ah-sid

**Moeritherium lyonsi** –
Moh-erry-THEE-ree-um lie-ON-see

**Mustellid** –
mus-TELL-id

**Oxyaena lupina** –
Oxee-AYN-ah loo-PEE-na

**Panthera spelaea** –
Pan-THEE-rah spel-AY-ah

**Palaeomeryx kaupi** –
Pay-lee-oh-MER-iks kah-oo-pee

**Paleolagus** –
Pay-ee-oh-LAH-guss

**Phenacodus primaevus** –
Fen-ah-CODE-us pry-MEE-vus

**Platybelodon grangeri** –
Platt-ee-BELL-oh-don GRAYN-jer-eye

**Pleistocene** –
PLY-stow-SEEN

**Procoptodon** –
Pro-KOP-toe-DON

**Protosiren** –
Proh-toe-SI-ren

**Pyrotherium** –
Pie-roh-THEE-ree-um

**Stenomylus** –
Sten-oh-MY-luss

**Synthetoceras** –
Sin-the-TOSS-eras

**Titanotheridae** –
Titan-oh-THEE-rid-ee

**Thylacosmilus atrox** –
Thigh-la-do-SMILE-us AY-trox

**Toxodon** –
Tox-oh-Don

**Uintatherium mirabile** –
WINT-a-THEE-ree-um mi-RAB-ill-ee

**Ursus spelaeus** –
Er-SUSS spel-AY-uss